### A Guide for Using

# The Giver

### in the Classroom

*Based on the novel written by Lois Lowry*

*This guide written by* ***Pam Koogler*** *and* ***Carol Foell, M.A.***

***Teacher Created Resources***
6421 Industry Way
Westminster, CA 92683
www.teachercreated.com
**ISBN: 978-1-55734-542-4**

Reprinted, 2015
Made in U.S.A.

***Edited by***
*Cathy Gilbert*
***Illustrated by***
*Kathy Bruce*
***Cover Art by***
*Sue Fullam*

# Table of Contents

# Introduction

Good books are wonderful! They stimulate our imaginations, inform our minds, inspire our higher selves, and fill our time with magic. With good books, we are never lonely or bored. And a good book only gets better with time, because each reading brings us new meaning. Each new story is a treasure to cherish forever.

In Literature Units, we take great care to select books that will become treasured friends for life.

Teachers using this unit will find the following features to supplement their own valuable ideas.

- Sample Lesson Plans
- Pre-reading Activities
- Biographical Sketch and Picture of the Author
- Book Summary
- Vocabulary Lists and Suggested Vocabulary Activities
- Chapters grouped for study, with sections including:
  - — *quizzes*
  - — *hands-on projects*
  - — *cooperative learning activities*
  - — *cross-curriculum connections*
  - — *extensions into the readers' lives*
- Post-reading Activities
- Book Report Ideas
- Research Idea
- Culminating Activities
- Three Different Options for Unit Tests
- Bibliography of Related Reading
- Answer Key

We are confident that this unit will be a valuable addition to your literature planning and that as you use our ideas, your students will learn to treasure the stories to which you introduce them.

# Sample Lesson Plan

Each of the lessons below can take from one to several days to complete.

## LESSON 1

- Introduce and complete some or all of the pre-reading activities. (page 5)
- Read About the Author with your students. (page 6)
- Read the book summary with your students. (page 7)
- Introduce the vocabulary list for Section 1. (page 8)

## LESSON 2

- Read chapters 1–5.
- Choose a vocabulary activity. (page 9)
- Write news articles. (page 11)
- Design advertisements. (page 12)
- Diagram community judicial system. (page 13)
- Begin Reading Response Journals. (page 14)
- Administer Section 1 quiz. (page 10)
- Introduce vocabulary for Section 2. (page 8)

## LESSON 3

- Read chapters 6–10.
- Choose a vocabulary activity. (page 9)
- Complete a book of rules. (page 17)
- Play the career game. (page 18)
- Produce food without water and sun. (page 19)
- Learn all about bicycles. (page 20)
- Write in Reading Response Journals. (pages 14–15)
- Administer Section 2 quiz. (page 16)
- Introduce vocabulary for Section 3. (page 8)

## LESSON 4

- Read chapters 11–15.
- Choose vocabulary activity. (page 9)
- Complete "What's Wrong with This Picture?" (page 22)
- Discuss genetic experimentation. (page 23)
- Make a daily schedule pie graph. (page 24)
- Write a business letter. (page 25)
- Write in Reading Response Journals. (page 15)
- Administer Section 3 quiz. (page 21)
- Introduce vocabulary for Section 4. (page 8)

## LESSON 5

- Read chapters 16–19.
- Choose a vocabulary activity. (page 9)
- Complete the Cause and Effect Chart. (page 27)
- Examine self-esteem. (page 28)
- Debate "Release." (page 29)
- Share ideas about family duties and responsibilities. (page 30)
- Write in Reading Response Journals. (page 15)
- Administer Section 4 quiz. (page 26)
- Introduce vocabulary for Section 5. (page 8)

## LESSON 6

- Read chapters 20–23.
- Choose a vocabulary activity. (page 9)
- Create a community quilt. (page 32)
- Give examples of symbolism. (page 33)
- Brainstorm fine arts examples. (page 34)
- Discuss life's choices. (page 35)
- Write in Reading Response journals. (page 15)
- Administer Section 5 quiz. (page 31)

## LESSON 7

- Discuss possibilities for Jonas's later life. (page 36)
- Make a time line. (page 37)
- Assign book report options. (page 38)
- Discuss the Research Idea. (page 39)
- Take a field trip to the library for family tree research. (pages 39–40)

## LESSON 8

- Administer unit test. (pages 43–45)
- Discuss test answers and responses. (page 48)
- Hold round table discussions of student opinions and enjoyment of book.
- Respond in journals. (page 15)
- Provide a bibliography of related reading. (page 46)

## LESSON 9

- Generate ideas and share video presentation, "This Is Your Life, Jonas" (page 41)
- Discuss ideas for a mural and then draw it. (page 42)

# Before the Book

Before you begin the book *The Giver*, you can help your students to recall background information and stimulate interest by completing the following activities and discussing some of the questions.

1. Study the book cover thoughtfully. What do you think the title, *The Giver*, means?
2. Look at the picture on the book's front cover:
   a. Describe the man.
   b. What does the expression on his face indicate?
   c. What do you think the torn photo is about?
3. What if you were allowed to read only books chosen for you? How would that make you feel?
4. Does your family have schedules, rituals, or routines that are followed daily? What are they?
5. What happens when people do not obey rules?
6. Have you ever visited a place where you felt stupid or strange?
7. How far back can you remember?
8. Have you ever traced your family history?
9. Is it important to know your family "roots"?
10. What other books by Lois Lowry have you read? Do you expect this story line to be similar?

# About the Author

Lois Lowry was born in Honolulu, Hawaii. Her family traveled a great deal while she was growing up, and she has lived all over the U.S., as well as in Japan. She graduated from Boston University and later took a degree at the University of Southern Maine. In addition to writing for young adults, she is a free-lance journalist and a photographer. *A Summer to Die,* her first novel for young people, has been widely acclaimed and won the Children's Book Award. Ms. Lowry has also received the Newbery Medal for *Number the Stars* and *The Giver.* Ms. Lowry now lives in Maine and has two sons and two daughters.

Often Ms. Lowry, like other authors, is asked how ideas for books come about. Her reply is that there is no easy answer because her ideas usually come from memory, imagination, and special moments in her life. When specifically asked how she got ideas for *The Giver,* she answered that one idea came from a moment she shared with her elderly father. She recalls that while visiting him in the nursing home, he loved talking about his family because that was what he cared about most. Family photographs lined the walls of his room so Ms. Lowry and her father could revisit old times and share memories together. She noted that when he came to a particular photo of her sister, Helen, he could not remember what had happened to her. Ms. Lowry reminded him that she had died of cancer at a young age. Even though Ms. Lowry knew her father's memory loss was due to aging brain cells, she pondered the idea of a way to block out bad memories, to avoid pain, tragedy, and subconsciously remember only the good times. This experience became one identifiable source for the book that became *The Giver.* Lowry's fictionalized story of her sister is told in *A Summer to Die*.

Ms. Lowry answers these frequently asked questions excerpted from *Troll Book Lists for Middle School Readers:*

**Do you have a special method of writing?**
*It really just comes out of my head and into the computer. There is a lot of rewriting, but because it takes place throughout the process—each day I go back and rewrite the previous day's work—it is difficult to tell how many rewrites I do.*

**Is there a theme that pervades all of your books?**
*The most important things to me in my own life, as well as in my books, are human relationships of all kinds. Although my books deal largely with families, I also attach a great deal of importance to friendships. Those are the things that young people should pay attention to in their own lives.*

**Why are books important for young readers?**
*A book can be a vehicle for communication, and a book can alleviate the sense of isolation that sometimes makes growing up lonely. Walking through a scary place is easier if you know that someone else has walked there once and survived.*

# *The Giver*

*By Lois Lowry*
*(Available in USA, Houghton Mifflin, 1993; Canada, Thomas Allen & Son; UK, Gollancz Services; AUS, Jackaranda Wiley)*

This fascinating science-fiction novel is about a boy named Jonas who lives in a nameless community sometime in the future with no war, poverty, hate, fear, pollution, or disease—a utopian life. It is a world by itself with no choices at all. Each aspect of life has a prescribed rule: one-year-olds—"Ones"—are named and given to their chosen family; "Nines" get their bicycles; "Birthmothers" give birth to three children first and then become laborers; "family units" get two children—one male and one female.

Young Jonas is anxiously awaiting his Ceremony of Twelve, the time when all the twelve-year-olds in the community receive their assignments for their lifelong professions. Instead of being Caretaker of the Old, or a teacher or recreation director, Jonas is selected to be the next Receiver of Memories, the most respected of the Elders. The Receiver is a person who receives all the pains, grief, and pleasures in memories of the past. He takes the burden of war, starvation, neglect, misery, and despair. He also learns about joys that the community never experiences: They do not see color, hear music, or know love. He must receive all of the memories lodged in the mind of the old Receiver, whom he calls The Giver.

As Jonas is trained by The Giver, he discovers that he wants more than black and white, more than rules and security. He wants life. He desires color and choice. He wishes that everyone could feel love and pain.

The author gives you the feeling of being trapped and confused by breaking up the pieces and clues and scattering them throughout the book. You hit dead ends and curves as you are reading. Then, as pieces come together, new experiences are revealed, and instead of feeling trapped and confused, the reader may feel startled, sad, and angry. The cliff-hanger ending can be construed as allegory or reality.

This book is a lot like life. Our most cherished beliefs, the values of the individual, the family, and the society—these are the abiding emblems and themes interwoven throughout the novel. We take our way of living for granted. One day it may be gone; there would be no choices, no memories, no feelings or freedom. *The Giver* is a book that quietly and delicately reveals how important life is and suggests that, possibly, the way we wish life to be might not be the best way after all.

# Vocabulary Lists

The vocabulary words which are listed below correspond to each section of *The Giver* as outlined in the Table of Contents. You may want to make sure that students can pronounce and define words introduced. Ideas for vocabulary activities are found on page 9 of this book.

**Section 1**

*(Chapters 1–5)*

| | | | |
|---|---|---|---|
| intrigued | gravitating | apprehensive | ritual |
| adherence | abandoned | chastise | impatient |
| mystified | elders | chortled | nurturers |
| obediently | serene | insight | nondescript |
| ironic | palpable | transgression | infraction |
| aptitude | distraught | humiliation | remorse |

**Section 2**

*(Chapters 6–10)*

| | | | |
|---|---|---|---|
| reprieve | excruciating | indulgently | conspicuous |
| meticulously | exuberant | anguish | benign |
| integrity | independence | exemption | exasperated |
| relinquish | acquisition | scrupulously | crescendo |
| interdependence | integral | buoyancy | exhilarating |
| prestige | transgressions | indolence | deftly |

**Section 3**

*(Chapters 11–15)*

| | | | |
|---|---|---|---|
| torrent | perceived | admonition | relinquished |
| anguished | irrationally | ominous | meticulous |
| stench | fretful | tentatively | exempted |
| isolation | assuage | vibrance | parched |
| transmitting | consciousness | sinuous | imploring |
| unendurable | hueless | immobilized | carnage |

**Section 4**

*(Chapters 16–19)*

| | | | |
|---|---|---|---|
| luxuriating | faltered | risk | syringe |
| ruefully | imploringly | glimpse | expertise |
| ecstatic | pervaded | obsolete | wretched |
| solitude | hearth | permeated | dejected |

**Section 5**

*(Chapters 20–23)*

| | | | |
|---|---|---|---|
| mimicked | empowered | emphatically | stealthily |
| frazzled | instinctively | perils | obscured |
| hypnotically | lethargy | solace | languid |
| augmented | sarcastic | loomed | imperceptibly |

# Vocabulary Activity Ideas

Students can begin with the contextual vocabulary from *The Giver* and build upon it to use strategies for retaining, using, and extending their knowledge of word meanings. You may find some of these activities useful:

- Use a thesaurus to find **synonyms and antonyms** for the words.
- Try to use two or more vocabulary words to create complete **compound sentences**.
- Divide the words into **categories** based on whether each is a **noun, verb, or adjective**. Are any words left over? What category of words is left over? (Remember that some words may be used in several categories.)
- Circle **root words, prefixes, and suffixes.**
- Create an **illustrated dictionary** of all (or of a section of) vocabulary words by working together in pairs or small groups.
- Make a **crossword puzzle** out of some of the vocabulary words. Number the first letter of each word. Students write clues for the words, based on their meanings.
- **Scramble the letters** of each vocabulary word in a given section. Students then trade scrambled lists with each other and try to unscramble the words.
- Work in groups to **construct a bingo game board** with vocabulary words in each square. The groups then copy their boards and distribute them to the class for a bingo game. Group members call out definitions as players mark their game boards until someone yells "Bingo!"
- Using a selected list of vocabulary words, **play charades** by having students take turns acting out words from the list while the class guesses the words.
- Challenge students to use a specific vocabulary word from the story at **least 10 times in one day**. They must keep a record of when, how, and why the word was used.
- Play **"Malaprop Mania."** In groups students write a paragraph containing one or more words sounding similar to, but differing in meaning from, the assigned vocabulary words (examples: *languish* for anguish, *redemption* for exemption, *deafly* for deftly, *injected* for dejected, *ecstatic* for static). The group then exchanges paragraphs with other groups to see whether they can detect and correct the malapropisms. Prizes may be considered for the cleverest or funniest substitutions.

# Quiz Time

Answer the following questions, using complete sentences.

1. Who is the main character in the story?

   _______________________________________________

2. Name the major characters introduced to you in this section.

   _______________________________________________

   _______________________________________________

3. What does being "released" from the community mean?

   _______________________________________________

4. Describe the setting of the story in Section 1.

   _______________________________________________

   _______________________________________________

5. Why was Jonas so careful in his use of language?

   _______________________________________________

   _______________________________________________

6. Give an example that shows Jonas's concern for precision of language.

   _______________________________________________

   _______________________________________________

7. Give an example of Asher not using precise language.

   _______________________________________________

   _______________________________________________

8. What is the significance of "dream telling" and "feelings" discussions that take place during the family unit morning and evening rituals?

   _______________________________________________

   _______________________________________________

9. List four or more rules that everyone in the community must follow.

   _______________________________________________

   _______________________________________________

   _______________________________________________

   _______________________________________________

10. In Section 1 we learn that all members of the community receive an "Assignment" at a certain time during their lives. What is an "Assignment"?

    _______________________________________________

    _______________________________________________

# Read All About It!

Pretend you are a reporter for the community and your job is to gather facts and report news as it happens. Write news articles on the lines below each of the four headlines.

1. Include information that tells who should attend the Ceremonies, what they are, and where and when they are held.
2. Include the names of people involved in receiving children and the names of the new children.
3. Describe new comfort objects, where they can be found, and how much they cost.
4. Report a problem that a family unit is having and tell how the Committee of Elders help resolve it. Examples might be: a new child crying constantly, an eight-year-old sneaking out to ride a bike, or an adolescent forgetting to take pills for Stirrings.

## The Community News

**Ceremonies About to Begin**

**Family Receives New Member!**

**New Comfort Object Now in Stores Nearest You**

**Family Seeks Help from Committee!**

# Let the Ceremonies Begin!

In the first few chapters of *The Giver*, you sense that the community is greatly anticipating and excited about the upcoming Ceremonies. Some members in the community probably work long in advance to prepare for the event.

With a partner or in small groups, pretend you are on the advertising committee for the ceremonial program and must plan ways to spread the word throughout the community.

Use plain sheets of paper to design posters, banners, and signs that would publicize the event.

On the advertisements, you should make sure to include all important information, such as **who** should attend, **what** the event is, **when** the event will take place, **where** the event is being held, and **why** this event is about to take place. Be creative!

Fill in ad idea information on the sample poster, banner, and sign provided. Then draw or paint your advertisements on appropriate paper or poster board.

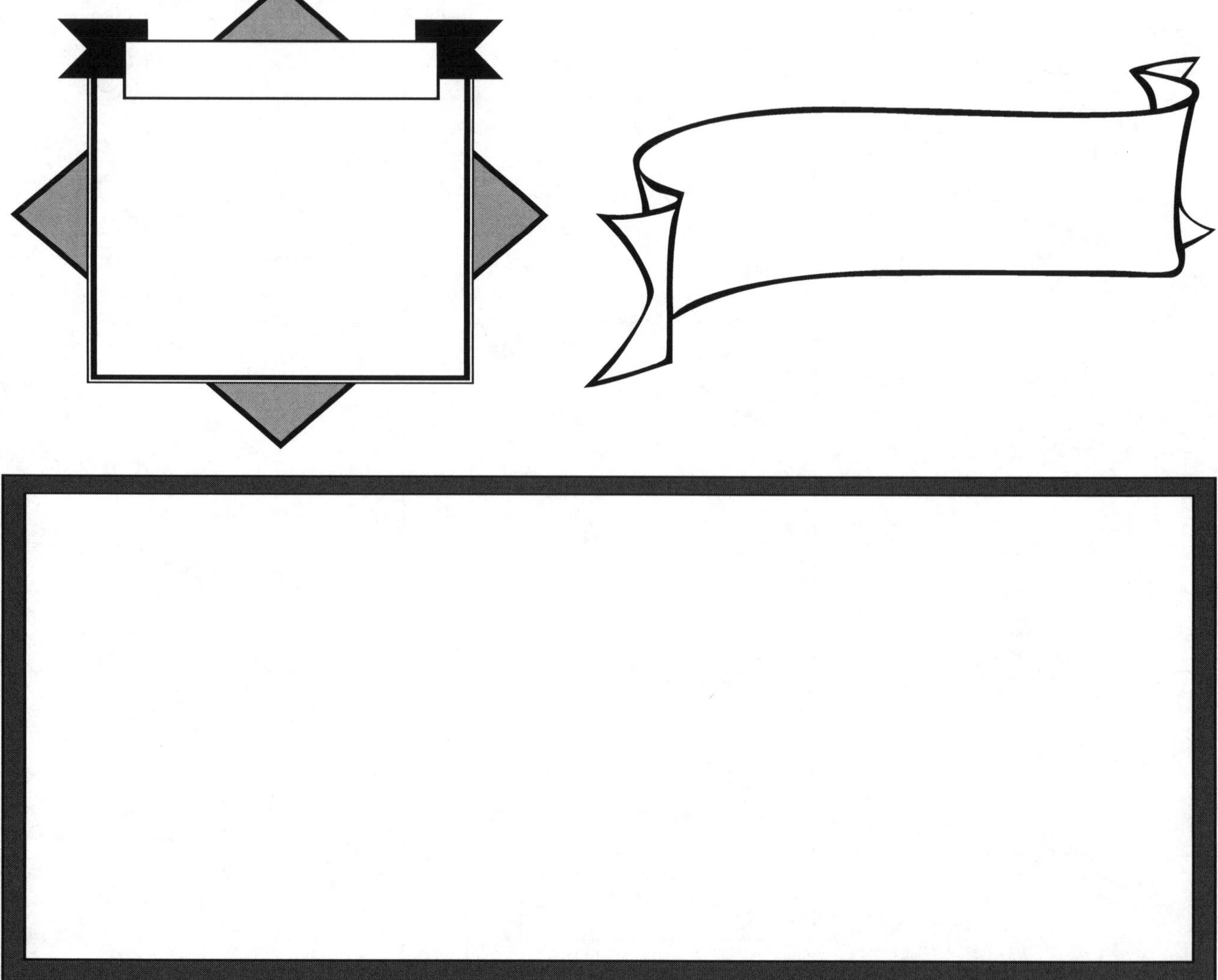

# Who Has the Power?

In the beginning chapters of *The Giver*, we find out that the community has laws, rules, and consequences for breaking rules. We are also told that certain members of the community have the power to rule over others. For instance, the Committee of Elders are leaders in the community who make the Assignments that determine one's future. We learn that Jonas's mother holds a very important position in the Department of Justice and is responsible for adherence to the rules. Also, there is mention of other committees and what some of their duties are. Finally, we learn that a person called "The Receiver" is the most important Elder, who makes decisions when the Committee cannot.

We know that the authors of the U.S. Constitution thought much differently about the use of power. Their idea was no one person or group of persons should seize power and control the American government. To make sure this did not happen, a system of checks and balances was devised under the Constitution. Accordingly, our government was divided into three branches—the legislative, executive, and judicial. The following diagram shows how this division of government works:

The community's system of government seems to be hierarchical in nature. If you look up the word "hierarchy" in a dictionary, you find that it means a categorization of groups of people according to ability or status.

**Activity:** Decide which community member(s) would be in control at the top (No. 1) and who would be taking orders at the bottom (No. 6).

Fill in the "hierarchy of power" ladder outline below. Unscramble and rank in order of importance or status the six groups of community members. The community groups are these: **committee members, family unit head—Mother/Father, Family unit member—son/daughter, The Receiver, Committee of Elders, committee head.**

1. ______________________
2. ______________________
3. ______________________
4. ______________________
5. ______________________
6. ______________________

# Reading Response Journals

Response journals can be one of the most effective tools you can use in your teaching of literature. Appropriately structured and written in daily, the journals can help even your reluctant reader to "get into" the reading by personalizing it for him or her and making it relevant. You may discover that after keeping journals, students will be able to focus better on what they read, and topics related to the reading which come up in class can be discussed more effectively.

**Teacher Directions**

- Tell the students that the purpose of the journals is to allow them to write how they feel and think about what they read.
- Before the reading, provide the question to be answered so that students will be able to focus their reading and give more thoughtful responses.
- Ask for a variety of responses, both written and graphic. Sometimes ask for responses comparing a character's feelings before and after an event to show cause and effect or comparing two characters to each other.
- Ask journal questions which relate characters and events in the story to students' own lives. Help them to compare what they read with life as they know it and to express their feelings about situations they have experienced.
- Write positive comments in the journals and grade them only for completeness and effort.
- Allow time for journal writing every day. If at all possible, keep journals in the classroom. This will ensure that they are always available when needed and will give your students the message that their writing journals are deserving of special treatment.

**Possible journal topics:**

1. The best memory I have with my family is . . .
2. Without my family, I . . .
3. My family roots go back to . . .
4. My ideas of a perfect community are . . .
5. If I were to run away from home, I . . .
6. Tell about any "good" memories you have.
7. Tell about any "bad" memories you may have.
8. A memory I would like to forget is . . .
9. If all people were the same race . . .
10. If I lived in a "controlled community" like Jonas, I would . . .
11. Compare the way the Old are treated in the community with the way older people are regarded in our society.
12. There are some references to "Release" in this first section. What do you think it means at this point in your reading?
13. The family shared their dreams every morning. Write about a dream you have had and what meaning you think it might have.
14. React to the description of treatment for "Stirrings." Do you think this means no one has boyfriends and girlfriends? How does this make life different?

# Reading Response Journals *(cont.)*

(Additional topics for Reading Response Journals or essay questions)

**Section 2** *Chapters 6–10*

1. There are more hints about what "Release" means (pages 48–49). What do you think it means? Give examples from the story.
2. The chief elder describes the life of children to age Twelve on pages 51, 52, and 54. Compare how the life and experiences of young children in the community are different from the experiences you have had.
3. List the qualities Jonas has that qualify him to be the next Receiver (Chapter 8). How does Jonas react to his "Assignment"?
4. Each dwelling in the community had only three reference books. (page 74) Jonas ". . . had never known that other books existed." Can you imagine a world without books? Which books would you miss the most? List your three favorite books and then compare your list with the list of another group of students.

**Section 3** *Chapters 11–15*

1. Write your reactions to the difference between "honor" and "power" in the community as given by The Giver. (page 84)
2 Comment on this observation that Jonas makes: "If everything's the same, then there aren't any choices!" (pages 97–98)
3. The life of the Receiver is very lonely. Why does the community need a Receiver? How would you feel if you were chosen to be the Receiver?
4. Chapter 15 is the shortest chapter in the book but may be the most powerful experience for both Jonas and the reader. Comment on what happens in this chapter and your reaction to it.

**Section 4** *Chapters 16–19*

1. Discuss Jonas's reaction to the experience of love (pages 125–126) and what happened when he asked his parents about love.
2. What impact is the baby Gabriel having on Jonas? How is Jonas affecting Gabriel?
3. Jonas has a strange reaction to his friends in Chapter 17. How does he feel and what decision does he "know with certainty" afterwards?

**Section 5** *Chapters 20–23*

1. Jonas and the elder have a plan that is " . . . barely possible. If it failed, he would very likely be killed." Comment on Jonas's motivation for even attempting this plan.
2. Do you think the story has a happy ending or a sad ending? Explain your feelings.

# Quiz Time

Write complete sentences to answer the following questions.

1. In this section why is the entire community going to the auditorium?

2. What is the significance of the "Ceremonies"?

3. What happens at the Ceremony of One?

4. What will Lily receive at the Ceremony of Eight?

5. What important object do Nines receive at their Ceremony? What does receiving this object mean?

6. How are the family units created in the community?

7. How does the family unit receive their children?

8. Name any occupations mentioned in Section 2 where math would be important in the community.

9. What story does Asher tell Jonas?

10. What are the responsibilities of the Committee of Elders?

# My Book of Rules

In the community, the people are given rule and instruction books after they receive their Assignments.

Pretend you have just been "Assigned" the career for which you volunteered and have just received your Book of Rules. Below, list the rules and instructions you would expect to find for your "Assignment."

You may want to refer to Jonas's folder of rules on page 68 of the novel.

## My Book of Rules

Name________________________________________

Assignment ____________________________________

**Rules**

1.

2.

3.

4.

5.

6.

7.

8.

*Special Instructions*

# Community Careers

In the community, everyone is eventually "assigned" a career to prevent people from making wrong decisions in choosing their life's work. Hold a class discussion about careers and have students brainstorm ideas about what they think it takes to be successful in the world of work. Through that class discussion, list on the chalkboard characteristics and skills common to most jobs.

1. Choose a career mentioned in *The Giver* and discuss what duties and services are required for that job. (For example, a Nurturer must be kind, caring, patient, and desire to work and interact with children. A Nurturer should have some pediatric medical skills and be a good communicator. A Nurturer should be punctual, neat, and have a flexible enough schedule to work any shift.)
2. List on the chalkboard all the different jobs the people had in the community. You may add other jobs that are needed in any community. You need to think of as many careers as there are students in your class.
3. On separate pieces of paper, write the different jobs from student lists. Number each piece of paper 1–30, depending on the number of students in class.
4. Fold pieces of paper and have each student draw one folded piece out of a container. Tell students not to show anyone else.
5. Give each student a 3" x 5" (8 cm x 13 cm) card and instruct them to write the number of the job and a job description, listing the duties and services performed by a given worker. Also include on the card the skills and personal characteristics needed for that career. Do not write the title of the job on the card, only the number of the job.
6. Collect all the cards completed by students.
7. Shuffle the cards and give one of the job description cards to each student.
8. Call a number from 1–30; the student with that number should place (with tape) his card next to the correct career listing on the board. (Repeat so students get a chance to match up different careers.)

| **Nurturer** | **Caretaker of Old** |
|---|---|
| | |

| **Birth Mother** | **Judge** | **Collection Crew** |
|---|---|---|
| | | |

 

# Make a Terrarium

Jonas's community had no rain, an element our society considers vital to the success of food crops. This activity will enable students to simulate the type of observation and experimentation that it took to establish the community in *The Giver*. The terrarium will display how food can be produced in growing chambers with controlled conditions, similar to a greenhouse or hothouse.

**Materials:**

- 2-liter soda container
- 2 tablespoons (30 mL) of water
- potting soil
- pebbles
- bean seeds: green/soy/lima
- carrot seeds
- bell pepper seeds
- lettuce seeds
- celery seeds
- alfalfa seeds
- duct tape

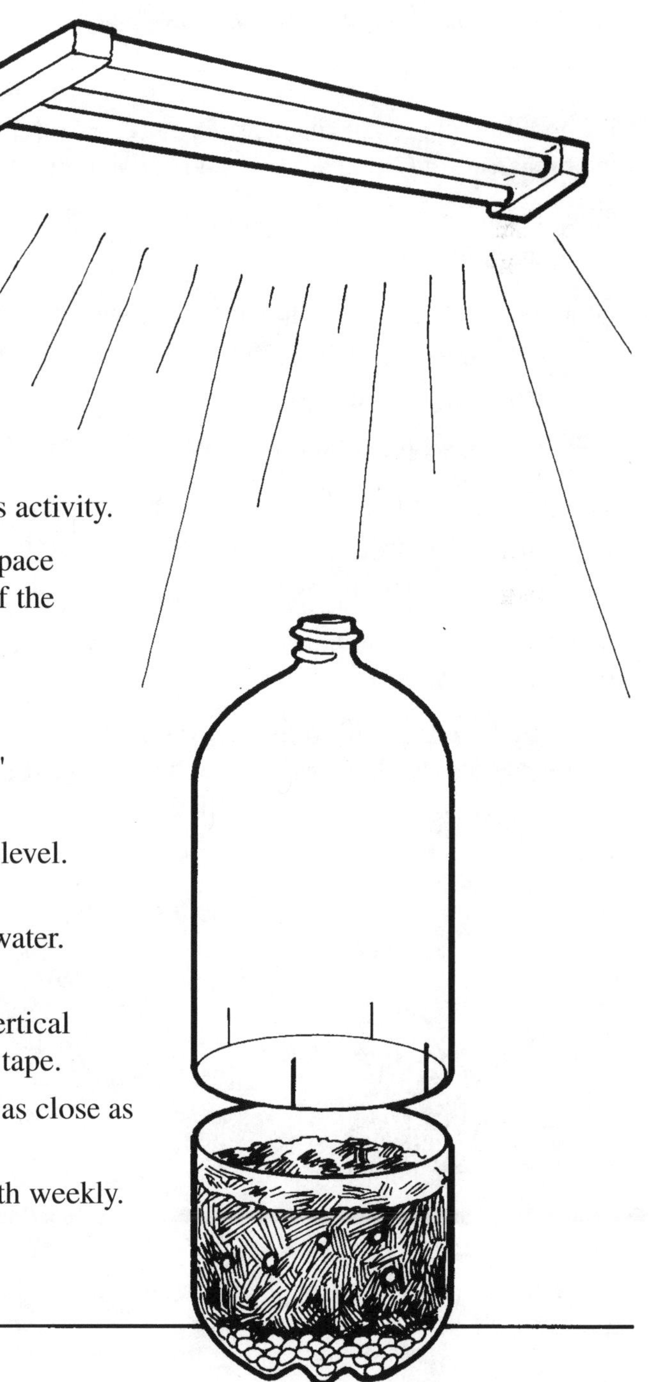

**Directions:** You may work in pairs to complete this activity.

1. Cut off the bottom third of the soda container. Space four 1" (2.5 cm) vertical slices around the base of the top section and put it aside.
2. Put a single layer of pebbles in the base of the container.
3. Add potting soil on top of pebbles to within 1/2 " (1.3 cm) of the top edge.
4. Plant seeds 1/2"– 1" (1.3 cm–2.5 cm) below soil level. Use 3–5 seeds per container.
5. Add one to two tablespoons (15 mL–30 mL) of water. Soil should be moist, not soggy.
6. Place container top back onto base, sliding the vertical slices down into the base. Seal tightly with duct tape.
7. Place terrarium directly under fluorescent lights, as close as possible.
8. Watch and monitor plant progress. Record growth weekly.

# Pedal Power

In the first section of *The Giver* we find that the people in the community consider the bicycle very important. All the children in the community receive a bike during the Ceremony of Nine. In Jonas's community you could probably imagine that the bicycle repair shop would be busy most of the time.

If you own a bike now, or if you know someone who has a bike, or if you would like to own a bike, how would you rank its importance? There are certain responsibilities that come with owning a bike. Would you take care of it? If it had a flat tire, could you fix it? Could you mend a broken chain? What if the pedals stuck or the seat loosened? Would owning a repair manual be beneficial? How?

**Activities**

1. Using a bicycle repair manual of your own, reference material from an encyclopedia, or a bike manual from the library, draw a poster showing the different parts of a bike and the function of each.
2. Give a how-to speech demonstrating how a bicycle works, how to repair a particular part, or how to make an adjustment on a part.
3. In an encyclopedia look up the history of the bicycle and answer these questions:
   a. Who invented the bicycle?
   b. Where was it invented?
   c. When was it invented?
   d. What are some different types of bikes?
4. What are some of the advantages of riding a bike in the community? List any disadvantages you can think of.
5. Are there any communities you know of where bicycles are the main form of transportation? Describe and explain why.
6. Decide on a type of bicycle that you might want to own. Describe the bike you want to buy. Call or visit several bicycle shops to determine the cost of a new bike. Compare the costs among shops and between buying a new or used bike.

# Quiz Time

Answer the following questions, using complete sentences.

1. What are some things Jonas begins to perceive and eventually begins to "see"?

2. How does The Giver feel after he transmits the first memory?

3. What does Jonas learn about climate control?

4. What does Jonas learn he is seeing in the apple, Fiona's hair, the faces in the crowd, and in the sled?

5. Where do you think the idea of "Sameness" came from, and why were there no differences in people other than gender and assigned jobs?

6. When Jonas learns all about colors, he claims "it isn't fair that nothing has color." Why does he say this?

7. From what are the people in the community being protected by not having to make choices?

8. What memory worse than "sunburn" does The Giver transmit to Jonas?

9. The Giver explains to Jonas that he will gain something by being the holder of memories. What will Jonas gain?

10. Why does The Giver ask Jonas for forgiveness?

# What's Wrong with This Picture?

Carefully study the pictures of scenes, objects, or persons below. Using the information you have learned through chapter fifteen, decide whether the picture is one you would likely see in Jonas's community. Under the picture, write *yes* or *no* and give at least one reason to support your decision. Use page numbers if possible. A sample answer for number one is given.

1. *No. You would not find an artist's painting palette in the community because color is unknown. There is only "Sameness," as The Giver explains to Jonas on page 94.*

# Talk It Over!

In *The Giver*, you learn that the community has "Sameness." Except for gender and some minor differences, the people look the same and consider it rude to speak of anyone's differences.

In small groups, discuss the following questions and have group members follow up with researched information that will give answers to the questions. Be sure to choose a person to record your group's answers to share with the class.

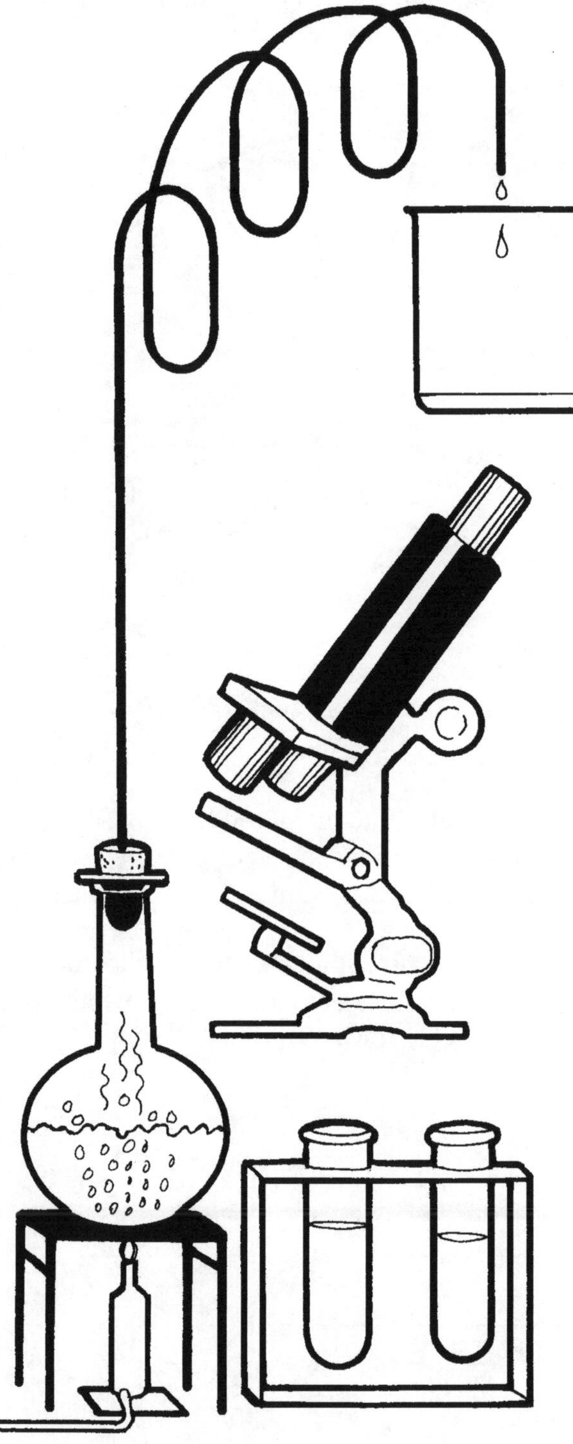

1. How could "Sameness" have come about?
2. Why would the community continue to have "Sameness"?
3. What is "genetics"?
4. Throughout history there have been accounts of genetic experimentation. Find out about any genetic experimentation that has been tried in the past.
5. Were the results of these genetic experiments good for humans, or were they a threat? Explain.
6. Have there been any genetic experiments, especially in medicine, where positive results occurred?
7. Do you believe that genetic changes will be used in the future for the betterment of mankind? Explain.
8. Do you feel that the people in our world are more the same than they are different? Explain.
9. Is there a chance that future humans will be the same? Explain.
10. Have our individual differences made us better? Would you want to lose your individuality? Explain.

# Daily Activity Graph

Like you, Jonas has certain things that must be done in a day's time with only so many hours to do them.

If we could see how this looks in a picture or graph form, it might give us a better idea of how to plan our daily activities, especially if unexpected events occur.

Suppose that Jonas's 24-hour day is spent in these ways: getting ready for school (1 hour), eating meals (1 hour), having morning and evening family rituals (1 hour), attending school (6 hours), volunteering (3 hours), doing homework (2 hours), having recreation time (2 hours) and sleeping (8 hours).

A pie graph of Jonas's day might look like this:

Could Jonas change his daily schedule?

_______________________________________

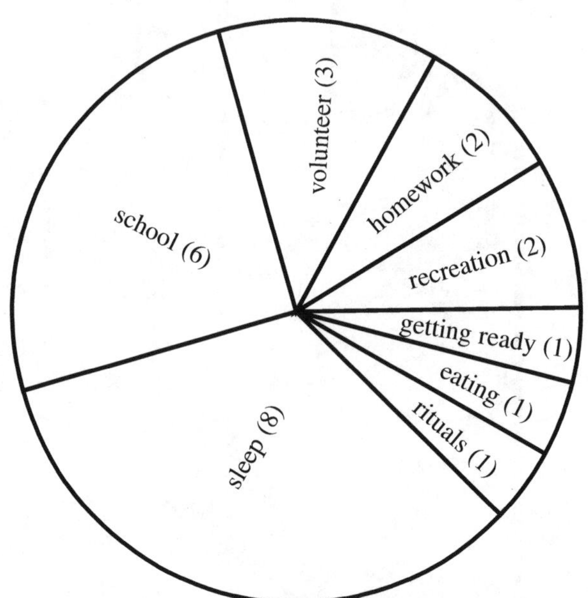


Make a list of things that you must do each day and the approximate amount of time it takes to do them. For example: If you sleep 8 hours and there are 24 hours in a day, what part of 24 hours is 8 hours? Answer: 1/3. Then 1/3 of your graph should be labeled sleep time.

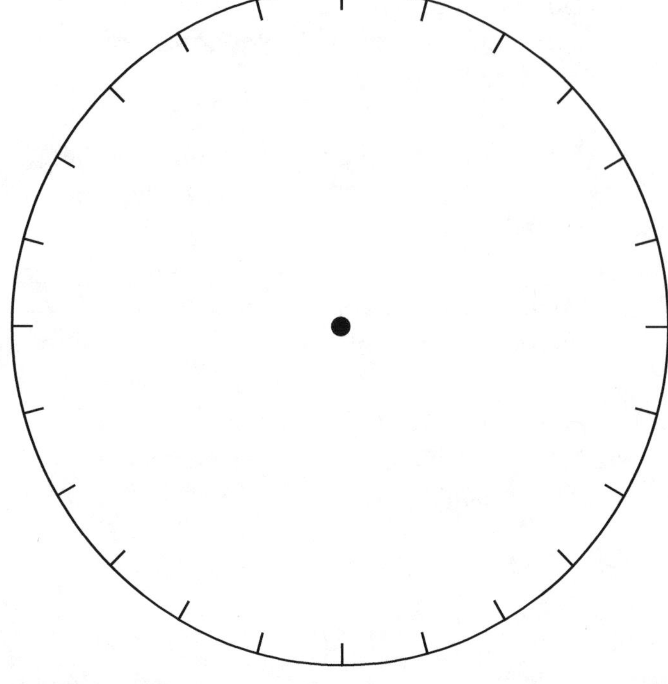

Now fill in the pie graph to the left with divided sections that will indicate your daily activities and the time allotted for each.

Are there times in your daily schedule where changes could be made to improve the day or provide fewer conflicts?

_______________________________________

_______________________________________

_______________________________________

_______________________________________

# A Business Matter

The people in the community are allowed to choose where they spend their "Volunteer Hours." Pretend you are a member of the community and would like some information about volunteering your time in The House of the Old. Write a business letter to the Director of The House of the Old, Central Plaza Building, The Community. Include your name, age, family unit, and any previous experience dealing with the Old. Tell why you think you would do a good job volunteering there. Finally, request information about the duties and requirements of the job.

Review the parts of a business letter shown below. Note the six parts, and then write your own business letter.

***Heading*** ______________________________

______________________________

______________________________

***Inside Address*** ______________________________

______________________________

______________________________

***Greeting*** ______________________________

***Body*** ______________________________________________________

______________________________________________________

______________________________________________________

______________________________________________________

______________________________________________________

______________________________________________________

______________________________________________________

______________________________________________________

***Closing*** ______________________________

***Signature*** ______________________________

# Quiz Time

Answer the following questions, using complete sentences.

1. After the memory of war, The Giver is gentle with Jonas, giving him tidbits of happy memories. What are some of these memories?

2. What is The Giver's favorite memory?

3. Where does Jonas learn he can find the names of his parents' parents?

4. Why doesn't Jonas want to play the "good guys/bad guys" game anymore?

5. What feelings does Jonas experience when he is given the holiday celebration memory?

6. Twins are not acceptable in the community. Why? What determines their fate?

7. Who was Rosemary? Why did she ask the Chief Elder for release?

8. After Rosemary's "Release," what happened to the community?

9. What does Jonas learn about what happens during a "Release"?

10. Can you think of a time either in present day or in past history when certain people have been "Released" for various reasons?

# Cause and Effect Chart

At the beginning of Chapter 16, Jonas does not want to go back to The Giver because of the pain he is enduring in the training process. He goes back because he thinks "the choice was not his." (page 121) By the end of this section, Jonas has made several choices, going against the rules of the community and the authority of his parents. This is a turning point in his life and in the novel.

In order to understand the impact of the experiences Jonas has had, create a chart listing the joyful and painful memories Jonas is given. Write his personal feelings and reactions to the experiences. Then extend your chart to show how Jonas develops certain character traits or changes as a result of the experiences.

"Trust the memories and how they make you feel." (page 125)

| Memory or Experience | Emotional Reaction | Character Trait or Character Change |
|---|---|---|
| war | overwhelmed by pain | can't play good guys/bad guys game |
| birthday party | happiness, joy | awareness of being unique, special |
| museum visit | | |
| horseback riding | | |
| walk in woods | | |
| oceans, mountains, lakes | knows there is somewhere else | |
| dreams after he stops taking stirring pills | | realizes a new depth of feeling for others |
| sees tape of his father releasing the smaller baby twin | | |
| | | |
| | | |

# How Do You Feel?

Self-esteem is an important part of one's personality. How you perceive yourself can have positive or negative effects on all you do and on other people around you.

Your friends and a loving family play an important role in molding a positive self-image. Only after The Giver's favorite memory transmission of a warm and loving family celebration does Jonas learn about the concept of love. But Jonas becomes confused after he asks his parents if they love him and his mother responds, "You have used a very generalized word, so meaningless that it's become obsolete." Jonas realizes that humans must experience all types of emotions and feelings, both good and bad, in order to "know" love.

Work in small groups in your classroom to discuss the following questions.

1. What type of self-image does Jonas have?
2. What would the community be like if there was "love"?
3. Would Jonas be considered inadequate in our society?
4. How would you feel if you or someone you knew felt inadequate compared to others?

**Activity:**

Imagine yourself in the following situations. Role-play the situations in groups of two to four members. Remember that the goal is to increase or improve a friend or family member's self-esteem. You want to encourage instead of criticize. You want to show that it is okay to lose. You want to try not to be judgmental about others or blame others for things you are responsible for. As a parent you need to send the message that loving your child is unconditional and does not change if a child fails at something.

1. You and a teammate are involved in practicing a volleyball skill for physical education. Your friend attempts to serve the ball overhand and misses. The ball goes under the net.
2. You are playing a board game with a younger sibling(s). You lose.
3. You are complaining to your parent that you failed a quiz in one teacher's class because that teacher is mean and does not like you.
4. Create an original situation that requires positive reactions to improve a person's self-image. Role-play the situation and share your observations with the rest of the class.

# Debate

In Jonas's community, people judged inadequate or uncertain could be Released, which meant death. Possible Releases included: the Old, people who broke rules, twins (the one who weighed less), difficult babies, and those who were said to be uncertain or inadequate.

l. Have students research *euthanasia*, the practice of painlessly putting people to death, or *mercy killing*, as it is also called in our society. Ask students to write a short paper presenting the research information. In the same assignment, have students compare euthanasia to *release* in Jonas's community.

2. Set up class teams with five members each to debate the pros and cons of release. Have teams debate the idea of mercy killing based on facts they have gathered in their research and opinions they have reached. Students not on teams will judge the debate and decide who wins the debate, based on their knowledge from their own research and how well the teams supported their arguments.

**Teacher Note:** Before the debate, announce to all students the amount of time they will have to debate the issue. You may want to present a question from the list below and give teams three minutes each to debate the issue. If you choose 10 of the questions to debate, the class time would be approximately one hour (three minutes per question per team times two teams times 10 questions.)

A student or teacher of a high school debate team could act as moderator to keep the debate focused, present questions, and alert students to their remaining time.

**Possible Questions for Debate**

1. Should the United States legalize mercy killing?
2. Why are you for or against mercy killing?
3. What are some reasons for or against mercy killing?
4. Can you foresee any problems in the future if we legalize the practice of euthanasia?
5. Can you foresee any problems in the future if we do not legalize mercy killing?
6. Were there times from the past when euthanasia was practiced? Were there consequences or not?
7. Can death be defined?
8. How do physicians decide when someone is dead?
9. Do people have the "right" to die?
10. Should families of terminally ill people be given the right to end their loved ones' lives?
11. Would you consider having a living will or not?
12. Have attitudes toward death changed from the past or not?
13. Should "death education" be taught in schools?

**Possible Resources**

1. *Death and Dying.* Ed. by Janelle Rohr. Greenhaven, 1987. Suitable for younger readers.
2. *The Last Dance: Encountering Death and Dying*. DeSpelder, Lynne A. L. 2nd. ed. Mayfield Pub. Co. 1987.
3. Hospice Association or local nursing homes
4. School psychologist, school guidance counselor.
5. School or community library, churches, or local clergy

# A Family Affair

In Jonas's efficiently run family unit everyone has duties, jobs, and areas of responsibilities. If each member of a family does his/her part, the family functions smoothly, but if one member slacks off, becomes discontent, and does not do what is expected, another family member must take over. This could create a breakdown in the efficiency of the family unit.

**Something to Think About**

1. Does each member in your family have duties or responsibilities at home?
2. Are each of these duties performed daily?
3. How much time is spent on each task?
4. Is there a more efficient way to do each task?

In the space below, list the duties and responsibilities for each family member for one day and record how long it takes to complete each one.

| Family Member | Daily Duties and Responsibilities | Amount of Time |
|---|---|---|
| | | |
| | | |
| | | |
| | | |
| | | |

**Results of daily recording:** Write about or discuss your observations as a result of completing this chart.

1. Is any one family member doing more or less than he/she should?

   ______________________________

   ______________________________

2. Are you satisfied with the division of labor? Explain why or why not.

   ______________________________

   ______________________________

3. When you grow up and raise a family of your own, will the division of labor be the same or different? Explain.

   ______________________________

   ______________________________

# Quiz Time

Write complete sentences to answer the following questions.

1. What does Jonas learn about what happens to the Old?

______________________________________________

______________________________________________

2. Jonas and The Giver decide that things have to change, so they think of a plan. Explain their plan.

______________________________________________

______________________________________________

3. Why will The Giver not go with Jonas?

______________________________________________

______________________________________________

4. What does Jonas want The Giver to keep for himself?

______________________________________________

______________________________________________

5. What things does The Giver transmit to Jonas to help him on his journey?

______________________________________________

______________________________________________

6. Who do we find out Rosemary really is?

______________________________________________

______________________________________________

7. Who does Jonas take with him as he escapes?

______________________________________________

______________________________________________

8. What probably would have happened to Gabe if he had stayed in the community?

______________________________________________

______________________________________________

9. What are some of the new and good experiences Jonas and Gabe have on their journey?

______________________________________________

______________________________________________

10. What happens to Jonas and Gabe at the end of the story?

______________________________________________

______________________________________________

# Community Story Quilt

A quilt is a good example of a finished product that combines individuality and cooperation. Create a class quilt for *The Giver*.

**Materials:**

- 12" (30 cm) square of drawing paper for each student
- 14" (35 cm) square of muslin (cut with pinking shears) for each student
- various fabric paints

**Directions:**

1. Ask each student to think of a scene or character from *The Giver* and draw it on the 12" (30 cm) square drawing paper. (The size of the paper is smaller than the muslin to allow for seam allowance when sewn together.)
2. When the students are satisfied with their planned drawings, give them the 14" (35 cm) square of muslin on which they should transfer their designs, using fabric paints. Students should sign their squares.
3. Arrange finished, painted muslin squares in rows to create a square or rectangular quilt.
4. For the centermost square, title the quilt (for example, *The Giver*, the class section number, and teacher's name).
5. Once the entire quilt is laid out neatly, begin stitching the squares together. This can be done cooperatively with the home economics class, by parent volunteers, or the students themselves. If sewing machines are not available, stitch by hand with a running stitch.
6. When the quilt is completely sewn, display it in the school lobby, library, hallway, or on a classroom wall.

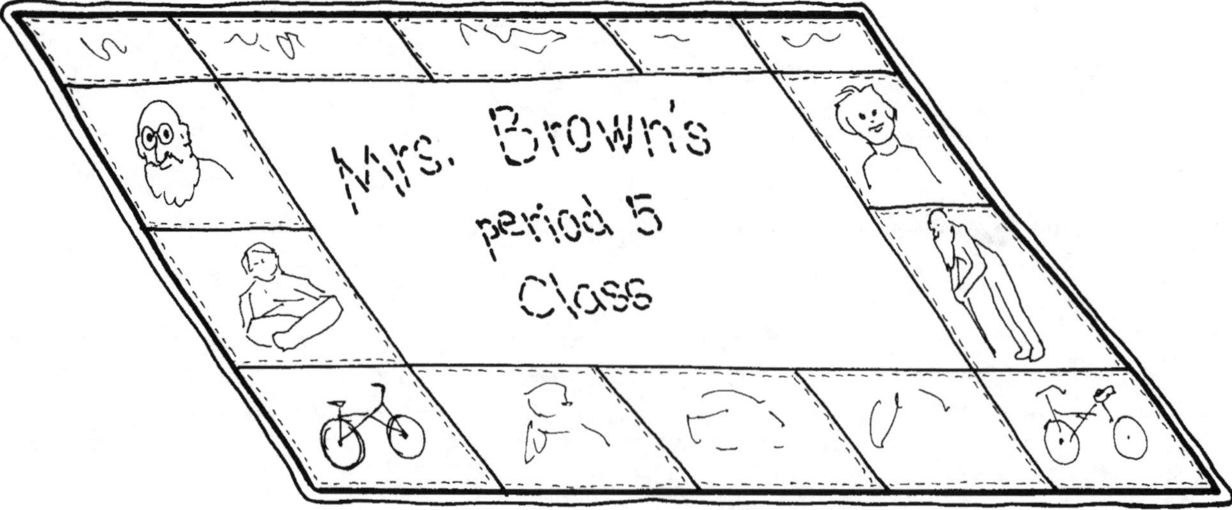


**Variations:**

- Have young children draw their designs on drawing paper with crayons or markers instead of painting on muslin. Then use a hole punch to punch holes along the four sides of their designed square. Have students lace their squares together, using yarn.
- Have community volunteers demonstrate and teach quilting techniques to the class and then use this type of hand stitching to join quilt squares.

# Symbolism

Symbolism is the use of a concrete or real object to represent an idea. It is a craft an author uses to make connections and clarify themes. For example, a bird, because it can fly, often symbolizes freedom. In *The Giver*, several examples of symbolism are used discreetly to signal stages of life that the community members are undergoing, particularly in relationship to the Ceremonies.

- Complete the chart by filling in examples of symbolism from *The Giver*. Then give examples of symbolism in your own life.

| Symbol | What It Represents |
|---|---|
| Jackets that buttoned in back for Fours, Fives, and Sixes | Interdependence and reliance upon others |
| Gabe's stuffed hippo and Lily's stuffed elephant | Comfort and love |
| Bicycles | |
| Hair ribbons | |
| | |
| | |
| | |
| | |
| | |
| | |

- List two or three symbols that are part of your life, and what they represent to you and others.

Examples:

| Symbol | What It Represents |
|---|---|
| Baseball hat | Fashion choice |
| Car keys | Independence |
| Nose ring | Rebellion, individuality |
| | |
| | |
| | |

# Music, Books, and Movies

Feelings such as isolation, depression, joy, hope, and love are themes that are often expressed in current popular music, books, and movies. Brainstorm for 15–20 minutes in groups of five to eight students to list some examples of popular songs, books, or movies that you know that might relate to the themes, experiences, and emotions that are part of *The Giver*. Some examples are listed to help you get started, but you will think of many others. Add any other themes your group has to offer. Compare your list with other groups in the class.

| Theme | Music | Books | Movies |
|---|---|---|---|
| War | | *Gone with the Wind* | *Born on the Fourth of July* |
| Love | | | |
| Family | | *Little Women* | |
| The Future | | *1984* | *Star Trek* |
| Friendship | | | *Stand by Me* |
| Independence | | | |
| Rebellion | | | |
| Running Away | | *Tom Sawyer* | |
| Utopian Society | | *Animal Farm* | |
| Courage | | | |
| The Elderly | | | *Cocoon* |
| | | | |
| | | | |
| | | | |
| | | | |
| | | | |
| | | | |

 

# Choices

After Jonas receives some memories, he makes choices that greatly affect his life, as well as his family and the rest of the people who live in the community. Would you have made the same choices Jonas made?

Describe how you would react in each of these situations.

1. You take an apple from the Recreation Center, even though you are not supposed to.

   ______________________________

   ______________________________

   ______________________________

2. You do not tell everything at your family dream-telling ritual.

   ______________________________

   ______________________________

   ______________________________

3. You teach your little sister how to ride a bike, even though she is not old enough.

   ______________________________

   ______________________________

   ______________________________

4. You want to witness a "Release."

   ______________________________

   ______________________________

   ______________________________

5. You transmit memories to a little child, even though you know it is wrong.

   ______________________________

   ______________________________

   ______________________________

6. You tell a lie to your parents.

   ______________________________

   ______________________________

7. You steal food and your father's bicycle.

   ______________________________

   ______________________________

8. You run away from home with a small child.

   ______________________________

   ______________________________

# Jonas's Later Life

When you have finished reading *The Giver*, you may feel so familiar with Jonas, a fictional character, that you would like to know about his "later life." Since imaginary characters have no boundaries, you may want to add details to Jonas's adult years. On the lines below, write any questions you want answered about Jonas's later life.

Alone or in groups, write your own original answers for your questions. Answer the following questions also:

1. Does Jonas ever return to the community where he spent his first 12 years?
2. How do the people treat Jonas if he decides to visit the community again?
3. How is the community dealing with "memory return"?
4. What does Jonas say to The Giver if he sees him again?
5. Does Jonas go to college? If he does, what does he study? If not, how does he make a living?
6. Does Jonas get married? Does he have children? Does he share his adventure with them or keep silent?

# Time Line

Construct a time line of Jonas's life beginning with the Ceremony of Twelve to after his escape from the community. Include 10 or more events on your time line.

Choose two events to illustrate. Use only black, white, and gray before Jonas's escape from the community and choose many colors to draw events after his escape. When all events have been completed and illustrated in the sections below, cut the sections from this page and paste them together in the proper order.

# Book Report Ideas

Preparing a book report does not have to be tedious, as the list of alternatives below should show you. You may decide to use one of the ideas below for your report on *The Giver*, or you may choose another method that interests you.

**Promotional Video**

Make video presentations promoting the most popular and newest books like *The Giver.*

**Dramatic Video**

Make a video depicting scenes from a book or have students take the parts of particular characters from books in made-up scenes of their own. (See the This Is Your Life, Jonas culminating activity at the end of this unit.)

**Poetry**

In your poem, you may want to use some of the vocabulary words that you learned as you read, or you may want to create more freely. See whether you can capture the spirit of the book in your poem. Remember that poems do not have to rhyme.

**New Book Cover**

If you would like to try your hand at creating a new cover, now is your chance. Do not forget to use the space on the front and back flaps to add information to your project.

**Character Diary**

Choose several important days at strategic points throughout the book. Write diary entries that Jonas might have written if he had kept a diary.

**Diorama**

Create a diorama for an important scene in the book. This is a miniature scene, using dried or living plants, stones, dirt, small figures, and background pictures, etc., to create a three-dimensional effect.

**Character Puppet or Doll**

Bring a character to life, using materials you have at home or recycle old materials to make a puppet or a doll.

**Collage**

Browse through magazines, looking for illustrations that remind you of characters or scenes from the book. Then cut them out and arrange them in interesting patterns on poster board or large pieces of paper.

# Research Idea

**Teacher Note:** Students with adoptive or unknown family history could choose a famous person from history to research.

In *The Giver,* the people could find out who their birth parents were in the Hall of Open Records but were limited in information beyond that. Jonas did not know about grandparents or relatives until The Giver told him about them through memory transmissions.

**Something to Think About**

1. Is it important to know about family roots?
2. Have you or any member of your family ever traced your family history?
3. What could you learn from knowing about your ancestors?

**Research Activity**

1. Collect what you already know about your family or what you know about the family of a famous person from history. Write down names, dates, places, and relationships to others because that is how you will be able to identify ancestors in historical records.
2. Go to your local library and ask the media specialist or someone at the information desk to direct you to the genealogy department. This is the place where you can find records or tables of the descent of a person, family, or group from an ancestor or ancestors. You may even find a specialized guide oriented toward ethnic, religious, racial, or national groups. These books will explain what resources are available, how and where to look for information, and how to record and organize that information when you find it.
3. Begin the study or investigation of ancestry and family history by taking notes and making an outline.
4. Make a diagram or chart showing your family history (family tree). Put your name or a famous person's name at the top and work backwards, writing family members' names on appropriate branches below.

(Use the family tree graph on the next page to record your information.)

# Research Idea *(cont.)*

Place family names in blanks. You may want to add family names further back than great-grandparents and add more branches as needed.

**Family Tree**

**Self**

**Brothers and Sisters**

**Father**

**Mother**

**Paternal Aunts and Uncles**

**Maternal Aunts and Uncles**

**Paternal Grandparents**

**(Grandfather) (Grandmother)**

**Maternal Grandparents**

**(Grandfather) (Grandmother)**

**Paternal Great-Grandparents**

**Maternal Great-Grandparents**

# "This Is Your Life, Jonas"

**A Video Presentation**

When you are telling stories on home video, it is a matter of choosing the right picture, of lingering on a single shot, of accenting scenes with a pan or a zoom of the lens. Instead of sentences, you are communicating with shots—individual units of visual and aural information. Through your choices and execution of shots, you tell your story on video. Everything you want to communicate has to be there. Viewers can see only what you show and infer only what you imply in the specific shots you choose.

**Content**

- List significant events, people, and objects meaningful to Jonas.
- Write a script for a narrator to present these events and people to Jonas after he has reached "Elsewhere."
- Some people from his life may speak their own tributes to Jonas.

**Production**

- Assign parts for the cast of characters.
- Determine the necessary props and costumes needed.
- Practice and rehearse the script.

**Video**

- Once you have decided on the content of your video, the next issue is how to shoot it. Style comes into play. How should you frame, or "compose," your shots? Should you shoot a closeup? A pan? A zoom? Or something fancier?
- When is the best time to zoom, pan, fade, and try out all the other irresistible buttons on your camera? Each has a distinctive way of accenting a shot and affecting the viewer's perception.

  *Long Shot*

  Covers a significant amount of territory from a distance and often serves as an "establishing" shot at the beginning of a movie or scene, to root the audience in a place and time

  *Medium Shot*

  Full-body coverage

  *Close Up*

  Head shots or closer, best used strictly for dramatic emphasis

  *Pan*

  Horizontal, hand-pivoted camera movement; alternatively, used as a transitional device to change focal points within a shot

  *Zoom*

  Gradual closing in or easing back from a given perspective; a highly powerful effect best reserved for rare, melodramatic, and shock purposes

  *Cut*

  An ordinary change of shots, as opposed to a fade or other transitional technique

  *Fade*

  Gradual emergence or dissipation of an image, from or to complete black (The fade should be used only to make a distinct departure from the established time and place.)

- Video the production.

**Presentation**

- Share the video with the entire class or show your production to other classes.

# Creating a Mural

Announce that the class will be creating a mural with each person adding a part.

1. Students sketch any idea they have for the mural on 9" x 12" (23 cm x 30 cm) manila drawing paper. They may choose to draw their favorite scenes, characters, or memorable events from the book. Students work at individual paces, and some will be ready for step #2 before others, which works well.

2. Once they have completed their practice sketches and are satisfied with them, they take them to the chalkboard/wall where the 12" x 15" (30 cm x 38 cm) roll of art paper is hung.

3. To transfer their practice sketches to the final drawing, the students simply choose spots for their drawings and redraw them in pencil on the art paper.

4. Markers, colored pencils, and watercolor paints should be available to the students at this point in the project.

5. Numerous students should be able to work at the mural simultaneously, each in his or her own area, side by side. All students should work cooperatively, no matter which stage they are completing.

6. The finished project appears collage-like with all the different scenes, characters, and individual interpretations. This class masterpiece should be displayed on a long wall in the school hallway, cafeteria, gym, front lobby, or library. (If possible, laminate the mural to protect it.)

- The entire mural can be created in three to four class periods from beginning practice sketches to coloring final drawings. With 10 or so students at the mural together, each working in a separate area, the project comes together quickly.
- You will want to have students working on other culminating activities at the same time in order to occupy them when they are waiting to go up to work once their practice sketches have been prepared.

# Test

**Vocabulary:** Choose the correct word for each sentence.

1. intrigued
2. apprehensive
3. Nurturers
4. gravitating
5. ritual
6. infraction
7. buoyancy
8. acquisition
9. excruciating
10. exhilarating

1. "At first it's ______________ : the speed; the sharp clean air; but then the snow accumulates, builds up on the runners, and you slow, you have to push hard to keep going."
2. "My swimming instructor said that I do not have the right boyishness or something." '___________' " Jonas corrected him".
3. Usually, at the morning ____________ when the family members told their dreams, Jonas didn't contribute much.
4. . . . the children rode their bicycles to the riverbank and watched, ___________ , the unloading and then the takeoff directed to the west, always away from the community.
5. . . . his mother told of a dream fragment, a disquieting scene where she had been chastised for a rule ____________she didn't understand.
6. . . . we retold many of the stories that we all remembered from his days of language__________ .
7. . . . they had been brought to the stage by the __________ who had cared for them since birth.
8. __________ , Jonas decided. "That's what I am."
9. Almost instantly the __________ pain in his hand had diminished to the throb which was, now, all he could recall of the experience.
10. . . . they moved on to other jobs, __________ toward those that would suit their own interests and skills.

---

1. vibrance
2. immobilized
3. transmitting
4. ominous
5. torrent
6. imploringly
7. agonizingly
8. faltered
9. unendurable
10. admonition

1. The memory was __________ brief.
2. The Giver looked at him __________ , Jonas stroked his hand.
3. One of Jonas's arms was __________ with pain, and he could see through his own torn sleeve something that looked like ragged flesh and splitting bone.
4. Now it was __________ . It meant, he knew, that nothing could be changed.
5. He could see a bright whirling __________ of crystals in the air around him, and he could see them gather on the backs of his hands.
6. "But you know, even __________ that tiny memory to you—I think it lightened me just a little."
7. He was very aware of his own __________ not to discuss his training.
8. . . . that they were satisfied with their lives which had none of the __________ his own was taking on.
9. He __________, not able to find the word he wanted.
10. It was not __________ as the pair on the hill had been.

# Test

**True or False**

1. __________ Jonas's mother had the assignment of agriculture study.
2. __________ Jonas received memories for a year.
3. __________ Jonas chose to do his volunteer work in a variety of places.
4. __________ Lily never talked much.
5. __________ The Giver was an old man.
6. __________ Asher's assignment was Nurturer.

**Fact or Opinion**

1. __________ Jonas believed that memories should be shared.
2. __________ Lily received a jacket at the Ceremony of Eight.
3. __________ At one time, The Giver had a daughter named Rosemary.
4. __________ The Giver gave the memory of snow to Jonas.
5. __________ The Giver felt he should stay in the community to help after Jonas escaped.

**Matching Characters**

| | |
|---|---|
| a. Jonas | h. Robert |
| b. The Giver | i. Jonas's Father |
| c. Lily | j. Committee of Elders |
| d. Jonas's mother | k. Rosemary |
| e. Fiona | l. Chief Elder |
| f. Asher | m. Benjamin |
| g. Gabe | n. Caleb |

1. __________ worked for the Department of Justice
2. __________ leaders of the community
3. __________ the most important member in the community
4. __________ Jonas's "funny" friend
5. __________ assignment was to work with the new children
6. __________ became the new Receiver of Memory
7. __________ had been The Giver's daughter
8. __________ left the community with Jonas
9. __________ Jonas's sister
10. __________ devised equipment for Rehabilitation Center
11. __________ in charge of the Ceremonies
12. __________ Caretaker of the Old
13. __________ released because he was old
14. __________ child who drowned in the river

 

# Test

**Put the events of *The Giver* in correct sequence (1–7)**

a. Jonas and Gabe make it to Elsewhere.
b. Jonas learns The Giver has many books.
c. Jonas is selected as Receiver of Memory.
d. Jonas feels apprehensive.
e. Jonas learns what happens in Release.
f. Jonas learns the memory of war.
g. Jonas has first Stirrings.

1. ______________________________
2. ______________________________
3. ______________________________
4. ______________________________
5. ______________________________
6. ______________________________
7. ______________________________

**Essay:** Choose two of the following and answer in well-written paragraphs.

1. *Expository—Process*
   Explain how memories, good and bad, were given to Jonas and tell how each affected his increasing "wisdom."
2. *Persuasive*
   Convince Jonas to change his mind about leaving the community.
3. *Descriptive*
   Write a descriptive paragraph about Jonas receiving the memory of snow.
4. *Expository—Compare/Contrast*
   Compare and contrast Jonas's world with your world.
5. *Descriptive*
   How does the author, Lois Lowry, use imagery to describe snow and war?
6. *Persuasive*
   The "discipline wand" was used to correct children. Do you think corporal punishment should or should not be used in schools?
7. *Descriptive*
   Construct a detailed characterization of the main characters in *The Giver.*
8. *Narrative—Personal*
   How would it feel to be a part of the community? What role would you like to have?

# Bibliography of Related Reading

Baker, Robert S. ***Brave New World: History, Science and Dystopia.*** Twayne, 1990.

Bomans, Godfried. ***Eric in the Land of the Insects.*** Houghton, 1994.

Boyd, Candy. ***Forever Friends.*** Puffin, 1986.

Bradbury, Ray. ***Fahrenheit 451.*** Simon & Schuster, 1967.

Bunyan, John. ***The Pilgrim's Progress.*** Retold by James Reeves. Peter Bedrick, 1987.

Burleigh, Robert. ***A Man Named Thoreau.*** Atheneum, 1985.

Christopher, John. ***The White Mountain.*** MacMillan, 1967.

George, Jean Craighead. ***My Side of the Mountain.*** Dutton, 1988.

Huxley Aldous. ***Brave New World.*** Harper Publishers, 1934.

Lisle, Janet Taylor. ***Forest.*** Orchard/Richard Jackson, 1993.

Lowry, Lois. **A *Summer to Die.*** Bantam, 1979.

O'Brien, Robert C. ***Z for Zachariah.*** Atheneum, 1975.

Orwell, George. ***1984.*** Harcourt Publishers, 1949.

Paterson, Katherine. ***Bridge to Terabithia.*** Harper & Row, 1987.

Silverberg, Robert. ***Letters from Atlantis.*** Atheneum, 1990.

---

**Other resources dealing with grief and teenage problems:**

Compassion Book Services 415-933-0830

Good Grief Programs 617-232-8390

Rainbow Connection 704-675-5009

Hospice Resource Center
Hospice of the Monterey Peninsula
P.O. Box 3084
Monterey, CA 93942
408-649-1772

Fernside: Center for Grieving Children
P.O. Box 89440
Cincinnati, Ohio 45208

# Answer Key

**Quiz 1** (page 10)

1. Jonas is the main character.
2. Mother, Father, sister Lily, Jonas, Asher, Gabriel, and Fiona are introduced.
3. "Released" means a final decision has been made about a person's future. It could be a punishment.
4. The story takes place when it is almost December in a town known as the community.
5. Community members were instructed to use exact language or suffer public humiliation and make apologies for misuse of language.
6. He finally uses the word "apprehensive" to describe his feelings for the Ceremony of Twelve.
7. Asher uses the word "distraught" when he means "distracted."
8. Family rituals are part of the rules of the community. They are used to clarify feelings and share experiences.
9. Each family has two children. Everyone does volunteer hours. No bragging allowed. No rudeness allowed. Bike riding not allowed until Nines ceremony. You must take a pill for "Stirrings."
10. Assignment is their role in the community for the rest of their lives, like a career or profession.

**Quiz 2** (page 16)

1. The community is going to the auditorium for the Ceremonies.
2. The Ceremonies are an annual celebration where the children of the community are recognized with significant step-up changes until Twelve. At age Twelve they are "assigned" roles in the community.
3. Infants from the Nurturing Center are assigned to their family units.
4. Lily will receive instructions for first volunteer hours and a jacket with smaller buttons and pockets (for her own small belongings, indicating maturity).
5. The Nines receive bicycles. It is a powerful emblem of moving gradually out into the community, away from the protective family unit.
6. Couples apply for children—one male and one female—when they feel ready or prepared to become a family. Children are received, one at a time, several years apart, at the Ceremony of Ones.
7. Couples receive children at the Ceremony of Ones.
8. Accept any reasonable answer.
9. Asher tells Jonas about the boy who did not like his "assignment," so he ran away by swimming across the river to leave the community.
10. The Elders watch over the children during volunteer hours, assign roles, and make decisions about rules in the community.

**Quiz 3** (page 21)

1. Jonas begins to see colors, snow, a sled, a hill, and a rainbow.
2. The Giver feels slightly relieved from the burden.
3. Inclement weather limits crop growing time, makes transportation impossible at times, and slows everything down.
4. Jonas learns he is seeing the color red.
5. Accept any reasonable answer.
6. Compared to the colorless community, Jonas feels that color adds a vibrancy that all community members should share.
7. The people were being protected from the stress and pressure of decision making. They were perhaps being protected from the pain of making the wrong decisions.
8. The memory of a painful leg injury was worse than the memory of the sunburn.
9. The Giver says Jonas will gain wisdom.
10. The Giver asks Jonas's forgiveness for the memory of "war."

**Quiz 4** (page 26)

1. Some of the memories are a birthday party, museum visits, riding a horse, and a campfire in the woods.
2. The Giver's favorite memory is a happy, warm, holiday celebration with family that includes brightly wrapped packages, colorful decorations, wonderful kitchen smells, a dog lying by the fire, and snow outside.
3. Jonas finds the names of his parents' parents in the Hall of Open Records.
4. It reminds him of the "war" memory.
5. Jonas experiences love, warmth, and happiness.
6. Twins would look alike, and this would cause confusion and more births than are permitted. The one who weighs the most is kept.

# Answer Key *(cont.)*

**Quiz 4** (cont.)

7. Rosemary was the former "Receiver of Memory." She did not have enough courage to handle the pressure.
8. The community had to take on the burden of memories she had already received from The Giver.
9. The "released" victim is given a lethal injection.
10. Accept any reasonable answer.

**Quiz 5** (page 31)

1. Jonas learns that the Old are killed when they are released.
2. Jonas will escape the community, taking all memories that The Giver has already transmitted to him.
3. He must be available to help the community when memories start to return, and he also wants to join Rosemary.
4. Jonas wants The Giver to keep the memory of music.
5. The Giver transmits strength, courage, and endurance to Jonas.
6. Rosemary was The Giver's daughter.
7. Jonas takes the baby Gabriel with him.
8. He probably would have been released.
9. They see wildlife such as deer, birds, and a fox for the first time.
10. They make it to "Elsewhere."

**Unit Test: Option 1** (page 43)

Fill In:

1. 10
2. 7
3. 5
4. 1
5. 6
6. 8
7. 3
8. 2
9. 9
10. 4

Fill In:

1. 7
2. 6
3. 2
4. 4
5. 5
6. 3
7. 10
8. 1
9. 8
10. 9

**Unit Test: Option 2** (page 44)

True or False:

1. F
2. T
3. T
4. F
5. T
6. F

Fact or Opinion

1. O
2. F
3. F
4. F
5. O

Matching Characters

1. d
2. j
3. b
4. f
5. i
6. a
7. k
8. g
9. c
10. m
11. l
12. e
13. h
14. n

**Unit Test: Option 3** (page 45)

Sequence:

a. 7
b. 4
c. 3
d. 1
e. 6
f. 5
g. 2

**Essay Questions:** Accept any reasonable answer.

 